DEC 1 4 2016

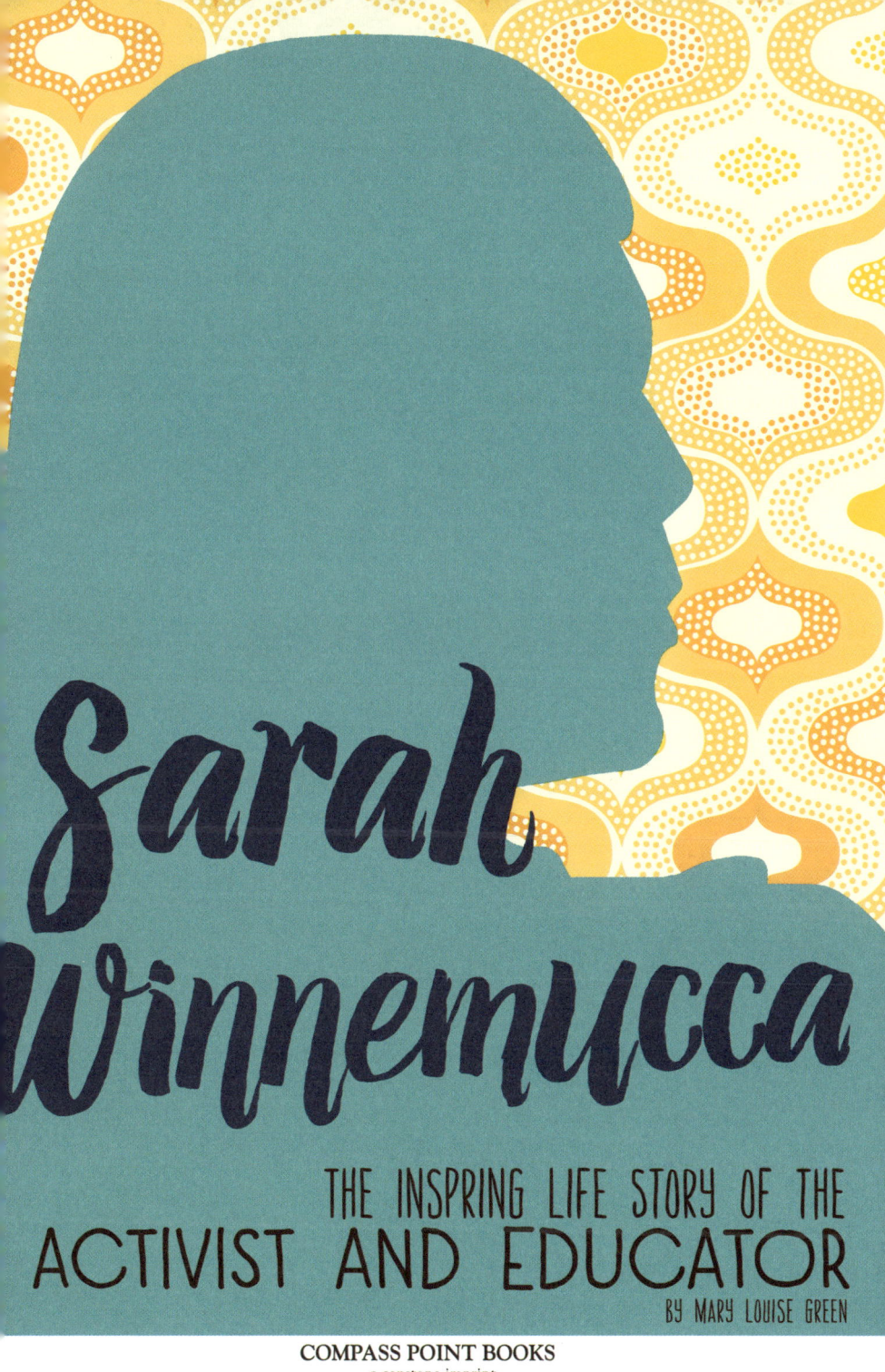

Compass Point Books are published by Capstone,
1710 Roe Crest Drive, North Mankato, Minnesota 56003
www.mycapstone.com

Copyright © 2017 by Compass Point Books, a Capstone imprint.
All rights reserved. No part of this publication may be reproduced in whole
or in part, or stored in a retrieval system, or transmitted in any form or by
any means, electronic, mechanical, photocopying, recording, or otherwise,
without written permission of the publisher.

Editorial Credits
Catherine Neitge and Angela Kaelberer, editors; Ashlee Suker, designer;
Wanda Winch, media researcher; Kathy McColley, production specialist

Photo Credits
Bridgeman Images: Brooklyn Museum of Art, New York, USA/Charles Loring Elliot, 14; Capstone, 54, 74; Courtesy of the Bancroft Library, University of California, Berkeley [F870.E3.B219], 36; Courtesy of the Nevada State Library and Archives, 38, 89; Courtesy of Ryan McGinness, 90; Dreamstime: Bjoern Alberts, 16, Neillockhart, 24; Getty Images: Bettmann, 95, Corbis/Scott T. Smith, 28, Transcendental Graphics, 81; Granger, NYC – All rights reserved, 4, 9, 21, 41, 58; Library of Congress: Prints and Photographs Division, 48, 69, 72; National Archives and Records Administration (NARA), 35, 56, 87; Nevada Historical Society, 7, 13, 23, 26, 31, 33, 43, 46, 53, 64, 66, 76, 83, 85, 93, 96, 102, 103, 104, 105; Newscom: akg-images, 99; North Wind Picture Archives, 10; Oregon Historical Society, OrHi-3866, 61, Oregon Historical Society, OrHi-56820, 63; Ronald M. James, Nevada State Historic Preservation Officer, 101; Public domain image found on Historic Oregon Newspapers, [illustration from The Sunday Oregonian, August 5, 1906], 71; Sarah Winnemucca, from "The San Francisco Illustrated Wasp," 1879, December 13, vol. 4, no. 176, courtesy, California Historical Society, FN-28234, 45; Shutterstock: kidstudio852, abstract design element

Library of Congress Cataloging-in-Publication Data
Names: Green, Mary Louise, author.
Title: Sarah Winnemucca : the inspiring life story of the activist and educator / by Mary Louise Green.
Description: North Mankato, Minnesota : Compass Point Books, [2017]
Series: CPB grades 4-8. Inspiring stories | Includes bibliographical references and index. | Audience: Grades 4-6.
Identifiers: LCCN 2016019212
ISBN 9780756551674 (library binding)
ISBN 9780756551896 (ebook pdf)
Subjects: LCSH: Hopkins, Sarah Winnemucca, 1844?-1891—Juvenile literature. Paiute Indians—Biography—Juvenile literature. | Indians, Treatment of—United States—Juvenile literature. | Women political activists—United States—Biography—Juvenile literature.
Classification: LCC E99.P2 G745 2017
DDC 979.004/97457690092 [B]—dc23
LC record available at https://lccn.loc.gov/2016019212

```
Printed and bound in Canada.
009644F16
```

Table of Contents

CHAPTER ONE
AN IMPORTANT LETTER................5

CHAPTER TWO
GROWING UP IN NEVADA................11

CHAPTER THREE
LIFE AMONG THE SETTLERS................25

CHAPTER FOUR
PRINCESS SARAH................39

CHAPTER FIVE
FIGHTING FOR HER PEOPLE................49

CHAPTER SIX
A STRUGGLE TO SURVIVE................57

CHAPTER SEVEN
BANNOCK WAR................67

CHAPTER EIGHT
LECTURER AND AUTHOR................77

CHAPTER NINE
LATER YEARS................91

TIMELINE................102
GLOSSARY................106
ADDITIONAL RESOURCES................106
SOURCE NOTES................108
SELECT BIBLIOGRAPHY................110
INDEX................111
CRITICAL THINKING USING THE COMMON CORE................112

Sarah Winnemucca would spend her life working on behalf of American Indians.

Chapter One
AN IMPORTANT LETTER

It was early in April 1870. Sarah Winnemucca sat at a table staring at a blank piece of paper. She knew the words that she was about to write would have great importance both for herself and her people, the Paiute American Indians. Sarah would have to choose her words carefully and express her feelings clearly. The lives of the Paiute people could depend on it.

Sarah was 26 years old and living at U.S. Army Camp McDermit in Nevada, just across the border from Oregon. About 900 Paiutes were living

Inspiring Stories

near the army camp. Because Sarah spoke English and Spanish in addition to several native languages, army officials asked her to work as an interpreter. She communicated between the officers and the many native people who came to the camp for supplies. She earned $65 a month—a decent sum at the time.

Before Sarah came to the army camp, she lived at the Pyramid Lake Indian Reservation about 300 miles (483 kilometers) southeast of the camp. At that reservation and at Walker River Reservation, the Paiute people were living in terrible conditions. They didn't have enough food, shelter, or blankets. Government agents from the Bureau of Indian Affairs were in charge of the reservations. Many of these agents were dishonest. Some took bribes from settlers or companies that wanted reservation land. Others sold the food and supplies that the government provided for the Indians and pocketed the money.

Major Henry Douglas, though, was a different type of person. When he took over as Indian superintendent of Nevada, he was concerned about

Sarah Winnemucca

A Northern Paiute family posed in front of their dwelling.

the condition of the Indian people. He asked Camp McDermit's commander, Colonel James N. McElroy, what he thought the government could do to fix the situation. McElroy went to Sarah and asked her to write a letter about the problems and possible solutions for people on the reservations.

Sarah wrote passionately about government policies and corrupt Indian agents who worked against the native people. She said, "If this is the kind of civilization awaiting us on the Reserves, God grant that we may never be compelled to go on one, as it is much prefferable [sic] to live in the mountains and drag out an existence in our native manner." She encouraged the government to consider giving the American Indians permanent homes on their

DOUBTERS

At the time Sarah Winnemucca wrote her letter, American Indian people didn't receive much formal education. Sarah's letter was so eloquent that some white people doubted an Indian could have written it. But many people agreed with what it said. A writer for *Harper's Weekly* said, "If it should turn out that there is no Sarah Winnemucca, and that no such letter was ever written, its statements will still remain as the plea and protest of thousands of the Indians."

In Nevada and California, local newspapers wrote both positive and negative articles about Sarah. They commented on her appearance and character. Major Douglas gave his own opinion. He said she was "passably good looking, with some education and ... much natural shrewdness and intelligence. She converses well ... and [uses] civilised customs, and will as readily join in an Indian dance."

Sarah Winnemucca

traditional lands where they could farm and attend school without having to worry about white people moving in and taking their land from them.

Douglas was so impressed with Sarah's thoughts that he shared her letter with officials in Washington, D.C. In May 1870 the popular national magazine *Harper's Weekly* published an article about Sarah and her letter.

Helen Hunt Jackson

Several years later, author Helen Hunt Jackson reprinted the entire letter in a popular book. *A Century of Dishonor*, published in 1881, examined the many problems that native people faced. Sarah Winnemucca had started on the path she would follow for the rest of her life—speaking and advocating for the rights of the American Indian people.

Explorer John Charles Frémont met the Paiute at a large lake he named Pyramid Lake.

Chapter Two
GROWING UP IN NEVADA

Sarah Winnemucca was born about 1844 near what is now Humboldt Lake in western Nevada. Her father, Winnemucca, and mother, Tuboitonie, named her Thocmetony. In the Paiute language, the name meant "shell flower." She became known by her American name later in her life. Her family belonged to the Kuyuidika-a band of Paiute. Her mother's father, Truckee, was chief of the band. Kuyuidika-a meant "cui-ui eaters." The cu-ui is a gray-brown suckerfish that was an important food for the Paiute.

Inspiring Stories

During Sarah's time, white people spelled her people's name in various ways, including the Piute, the Pi-Utah, the Pah-Ute, and the Paviotso. Today they are known as the Northern Paiute. Sarah's people called themselves the Numa, which means "people." The Northern Paiute lived in present-day western Nevada, northeastern California, and southern Oregon.

The first few years of Sarah's life were peaceful. She and the other children played near the lake, making small playthings from mud as their fathers fished for cui-ui or trapped rabbits for food. Sarah and the other girls wore skirts made of grass or tree bark as they learned to help their mothers skin the rabbits for clothing. They helped the women gather the nuts of the pinyon trees, which were a staple of the Paiute diet when roasted. She and the other girls also learned to weave baskets from grass and bark to store food.

The peaceful lives of Sarah and her people changed when white explorers and settlers arrived in the area where they lived. As Sarah later wrote, white people

Sarah Winnemucca

A Northern Paiute woman demonstrated in 1911 how pinyon nuts were cleaned.

"came like a lion, yes, like a roaring lion, and have continued so ever since."

Explorer John Charles Frémont was one of the first white people the Kuyuidika-a met. Frémont and his men met Sarah's grandfather near a large lake in 1844. Frémont named it Pyramid Lake because of a tower of rock that was located near its shore.

Inspiring Stories

John Charles Frémont

Frémont also gave a new name to Sarah's grandfather. He called him "Captain Truckee." In the Paiute language, truckee means "all right" or "good." Sarah's grandfather believed that the new ways brought by whites were good and would benefit his people. When Frémont returned to California, Truckee went with him as a guide. While Truckee was in California, the Mexican War (1846-1848) broke out. Truckee fought alongside Frémont against the Mexican soldiers. When the war ended, California became part of the United States.

When Truckee came home, he brought with him a paper he called his "rag friend." The Paiute didn't have a written language, so the act of writing a message on a piece of paper and relaying information to people across long distances was amazing to him. Truckee's "rag friend" was written by Frémont and told of Truckee's loyal service to Frémont and the United States. Truckee would carry this paper with him for the rest of his life.

While Truckee was impressed with white people and their ways, others in the tribe had different feelings. Many Paiute were afraid of white people. There had been some violent arguments earlier over land and river use. But these disagreements were not what most upset the Paiutes.

The Kuyuidika-a and other Paiute bands heard the terrible story about the Donner Party of settlers. During the hard winter of 1846–1847, the Donner Party was trapped in the Sierra Nevada on their way to California. During the four months that the party was stuck in the mountains, many of them died from disease and starvation. Some of the members of the party resorted to eating their dead companions in

Inspiring Stories

The Sierra Nevada is the Northern Paiute's traditional homeland.

order to survive. This story horrified the Indians, who sometimes made their children behave by telling them that the white people would kidnap them and eat them if they weren't good. This fear led to a terrifying experience for young Sarah.

One day when Sarah was about 4 years old, she was gathering pinyon nuts with her mother, aunt, and cousins. Word came that white men were near. The women believed they had to flee for their lives.

Sarah Winnemucca

Sarah and one of her cousins couldn't run fast enough to keep up with the rest. Their mothers had babies in their arms, so couldn't carry the older girls. The women decided they had to leave Sarah and her cousin behind. To keep them safe, they buried both girls up to their necks in the ground.

The women put sagebrush over the girls' faces to protect them from the sun and told them not to make a sound, or the white men would find them. Sarah said she never forgot how it felt to lie there all day, with her "heart throbbing, and not daring to breathe." Neither Sarah nor her cousin dared to even whisper. Late that night their mothers returned to rescue the terrified girls.

Sarah's fear of white people was well established by the time her grandfather, Truckee, returned from fighting in the Mexican War. Sarah was upset when she heard Truckee's plans. He wanted his family to go with him to California and live among the white people to learn their ways. Sarah wasn't the only one who was unhappy with Truckee's idea. Sarah's father,

Inspiring Stories

Winnemucca, told of a frightening dream he had for three nights in a row. He dreamed of huge numbers of white people coming into Paiute lands and killing the native people. He said, "They were killing my people with something that made a great noise like thunder and lightning, and I saw the blood streaming from the mouths of my men that lay all around me. I saw it as if it was real."

But Winnemucca's horrible vision didn't change Truckee's mind. Even the murder of one of his sons by white men fishing in the Humboldt River didn't change his good opinion of white people.

Around 1850 Truckee left for California with a group of about 30 band members, including Tuboitonie and her children. Winnemucca refused to go. Six-year-old Sarah rode on a horse behind her older brother Tom. Her brother Natchez, older sister, Mary, and baby sister, Elma, were also on the trip.

Sarah cried and hid whenever the group met white settlers. She begged her mother and grandfather to take her home. Only a sudden illness made Sarah change her mind about white people.

Sarah had touched a harmful plant called poison oak. Her face and body swelled and she had a high fever. Tuboitonie and Truckee didn't know what to do to help her. A white woman knew what to do, and she nursed Sarah back to health. This woman's young daughter had recently died, and taking care of Sarah helped heal some of her grief. She even gave Sarah some of her daughter's dresses. However, Sarah wasn't allowed to keep the pretty clothes. It was Paiute custom that anything that had belonged to a dead person must be destroyed, so the

OWL PEOPLE

Sarah's father, Winnemucca, called the first white men he saw "owls." He thought the white men's round eyes, pale skin, and beards made them look like owls. The term didn't help Sarah's fear of white people. Misbehaving Paiute children were told a story about an evil spirit called a Cannibal Owl. The evil owl spirit was said to grab bad children at night, take them away, and eat them. With the stories about the Donner Party and the Cannibal Owl in her head, Sarah was sure that the white people would kidnap her and eat her.

dresses had to be burned. Still, Sarah learned from the experience that white people could be good and kind.

When Truckee's group reached California, they found many more white people had moved there. In 1848 settler James Marshall discovered gold at Sutter's Mill in California. By 1849 thousands of people were pouring into California hoping to strike it rich. Towns sprang up almost overnight and grew rapidly. When Sarah's family came near Stockton, California, at night, she recalled seeing "something like stars away ahead of us." The lights of the town of 2,500 people were dazzling to Sarah.

From Stockton, the group traveled up the San Joaquin River to a ranch owned by Hiram Scott and Jacob Bonsall. The ranch owners hired Truckee and the other men as cowboys to train and care for horses. Sarah's two brothers worked on a ferry crossing on the river. The women, including Sarah's mother and sister Mary, worked in the ranch's kitchen. Sarah helped the women in the kitchen and started to learn words in both Spanish and English from other workers at the

Thousands of people moved to California in search of gold.

ranch. Not everyone at the ranch was kind, however. Some of the cowboys tried to assault Mary while the Paiute men were away. Night after night, Mary had to hide to avoid their attacks. Tuboitonie and the younger girls hid with her, moving from one small building on the ranch to another. It was a terrifying experience that they never forgot.

At the end of the ranching season, Sarah's family returned to Nevada with the money they had earned, along with beef from the ranch. Near the Carson River, they met some people who told them a frightening story. Many of the Kuyuidika-a, including two of Sarah's aunts and many of their children, had died of a terrible disease unknown to the Paiutes. Some Paiutes believed that white settlers had poisoned the Humboldt River. They wanted to attack the settlers in revenge for their peoples' deaths. But Truckee didn't believe the river had been poisoned. He correctly assumed that a disease had killed the Paiutes. It may have been measles or the deadly disease cholera.

Sarah and her family were saddened by the deaths of their relatives. But they were glad when they learned that Winnemucca and the rest of his band were safe, since they had spent the summer in the mountains, rather than near the river. Sarah was happy to be at home and have her family together again. But the situation didn't last long.

Life at a Glance

DATE OF BIRTH: About 1844

NATIVE NAME: Thocmetony (Shell Flower)

BIRTHPLACE: Near what is now Humboldt Lake, in western Nevada

FATHER: Winnemucca (1791?–1882)

MOTHER: Tuboitonie (?–1865)

EDUCATION: In household of Major Ormsby in Genoa, Utah Territory; briefly in convent school in San Jose, California; otherwise self-taught

SPOUSES: May have married a Paiute or white man in 1861 or 1862; married Edward Bartlett in 1871; married Joseph Satwaller in 1876; married Lewis Hopkins in 1881

DATE OF DEATH: October 16, 1891

PLACE OF BURIAL: Near Henry's Lake, Idaho

The mining town of Virginia City was almost named Winnemucca, after Sarah's father.

Chapter Three
LIFE AMONG THE SETTLERS

Sarah wasn't destined to live the rest of her life among her people. Sarah and her younger sister, Elma, were sent to live with Major William Ormsby and his family in the town of Genoa in 1857. At the time the town was in Utah Territory, but it is now located in present-day Nevada. Ormsby was a former soldier who owned a store and stagecoach station in Genoa. He and his wife, Margaret, had a 9-year-old daughter, Lizzie, who was about the same age as Elma. At 13, Sarah was a bit older than the other two girls. Truckee may

Inspiring Stories

Genoa was originally called Mormon Station.

have asked the Ormsbys to take the two girls to help them improve their English.

Sarah and Elma remained with the Ormsbys for about a year. It may have been during this time that Sarah adopted her American name. The two girls played with Lizzie and helped Margaret Ormsby with chores. While Margaret taught Lizzie her lessons, Sarah learned to read and write. Her English became excellent. She also learned about Christianity. Sarah liked the Ormsbys and the friendly white travelers she met at the stagecoach station. She no longer feared the "owl people."

But life for the Paiute people continued to worsen. A vein of silver mixed with gold was discovered in the heart of Paiute territory in 1859. This Comstock Lode was close to many pinyon trees. Once mining began, the Paiutes lost a large source of this important food.

Once the mines were running, thousands of white people moved to the area. They built a town near Sun Mountain in what is now Nevada. Some of the original settlers wanted to name the community Winnemucca, in honor of Sarah's father. The settlers considered Winnemucca a fair and respected leader. But newer settlers didn't support the idea, and the new town was named Virginia City.

The bitterly cold winter of 1859–1860 was a hard one for the Paiutes. Mining had helped destroy their way of life. Many of the animals they hunted for food had been killed or scared away by the miners. They

Inspiring Stories

Pyramid Lake lies within the Pyramid Lake Reservation, which is 35 miles (56 km) from Reno, Nevada.

didn't even have their usual supply of stored pinyon nuts to get them through the winter. Some starving Paiutes camped outside Virginia City and began to eat the townspeople's garbage to survive. Others stole cattle from white settlers. When spring came, the Kuyuidika-a met with other Paiute bands at Pyramid Lake for the beginning of fishing season. Along with fishing, talk of war began.

UNJUST ACCUSATION

While Sarah and Elma were staying with the Ormsbys, two white traders were found robbed and dead in the area. Arrows belonging to the Washoe tribe were found in both bodies. The Washoe leader, Captain Jim, admitted that the arrows belonged to his tribe but also said no one from his tribe could have committed the crime. The entire tribe was gathering pinyon nuts and was nowhere near the murder scene. Under pressure from Major Ormsby, though, Jim brought in three Washoe men, who were arrested and put in jail.

Sarah's brother Natchez and cousin Numaga spoke with the Washoe. The families of the jailed men begged the officials to spare their lives. The prisoners were supposed to be taken to California for trial, but panicked and tried to run. Militia soldiers then shot and killed the prisoners. Sarah and Elma saw the men being shot and were very upset. Major and Mrs. Ormsby insisted to the girls that the men must have been guilty. But later, the real murderers were caught. They were white settlers who had used Washoe arrows to disguise their crime.

Inspiring Stories

Sarah's cousin Numaga, who was also called Young Winnemucca, tried to persuade the Paiute not to rush into war against the whites. He cautioned them that the whites greatly outnumbered them and had powerful weapons. He might have succeeded in talking his people out of war if not for a tragic incident. Two 12-year-old Paiute girls disappeared while gathering food. Days later, their families finally found them, tied up and gagged, in the basement of Williams Station. Three brothers named Williams owned the trading post on the Carson River. The outraged Paiutes rescued the girls and killed two of the Williams brothers, along with three other men at the post. They then set the buildings on fire. This began what came to be known as the Pyramid Lake War.

A few newspapers included the story of the incident that had provoked the Paiutes, but most didn't. White settlers assumed that the Indians had murdered law-abiding white men in cold blood. William Ormsby led a volunteer group of about 100 men planning to hunt the Paiutes down and punish them. Ormsby had been a close enough friend of Sarah's father and grandfather that they had allowed him to provide a home for Sarah and her sister. But now he had taken command of the militia riding against them. The group wasn't well organized, and he may have taken command because no one else wanted to do it. The men were confident in their ability to fight the Paiute warriors, though. Some said they would have "an Indian for breakfast and a pony to ride."

William Ormsby

When the settlers reached Pyramid Lake, they found out that their confidence was misplaced. They walked right into a Paiute ambush. Led by Numaga,

Inspiring Stories

the Paiute warriors were skilled in desert fighting. They hid behind sagebrush plants and large rocks as they fired on the settlers. Nearly 70 white volunteers were killed—William Ormsby among them. Numaga carried an unusual weapon—a battle-ax combined with a peace pipe.

Sarah later said that her brother Natchez tried to save Ormsby's life during the battle. "My brother said, 'Drop down as if dead when I shoot, and I will fire over you,' but in the hurry and agitation he still stood pleading, and was killed by another man's shot."

Despite the Paiute victory, Numaga's fears proved correct. More than 700 soldiers from California arrived by June. They outnumbered and outfought the Paiutes. The U.S. forces ending up winning the short-lived Pyramid Lake War. But because Numaga had originally called for a peaceful solution to the dispute with the whites, he was able to negotiate a plan to have reservation land set aside for his people at Pyramid Lake and Walker River.

Sarah Winnemucca

Numaga was sometimes called Young Winnemucca.

Inspiring Stories

During the Pyramid Lake War, 16-year-old Sarah and her sisters probably stayed safe with their parents in the nearby mountains. Old Winnemucca didn't trust the whites the way his father-in-law Truckee did, but he didn't want to fight them, either. He also didn't want his people to move to a reservation, and was against Numaga's plans with the U.S. government.

By the fall of 1860, Truckee was very sick from an infection in his hand, which may have been caused by a bite from a tarantula. The members of his band lit signal fires on the mountains to inform other tribe members that they needed to come to Truckee's side.

As the Paiutes gathered around him, Truckee sent for one of his "white brothers," a man named Snyder. He told Snyder that he wanted Sarah and Elma to attend a convent school in California to continue their education in a safe place. He asked Snyder to arrange the girls' transport to the school. Snyder agreed.

Truckee told Winnemucca that he wanted him to be head chief of the Paiute people. He told his family

Sarah Winnemucca

Sarah's father, Old Winnemucca

that they shouldn't throw away his "rag friend," but rather, bury it with him. Then he died peacefully.

Along with the rest of the family, Sarah grieved the loss of her beloved grandfather. She later wrote,

Inspiring Stories

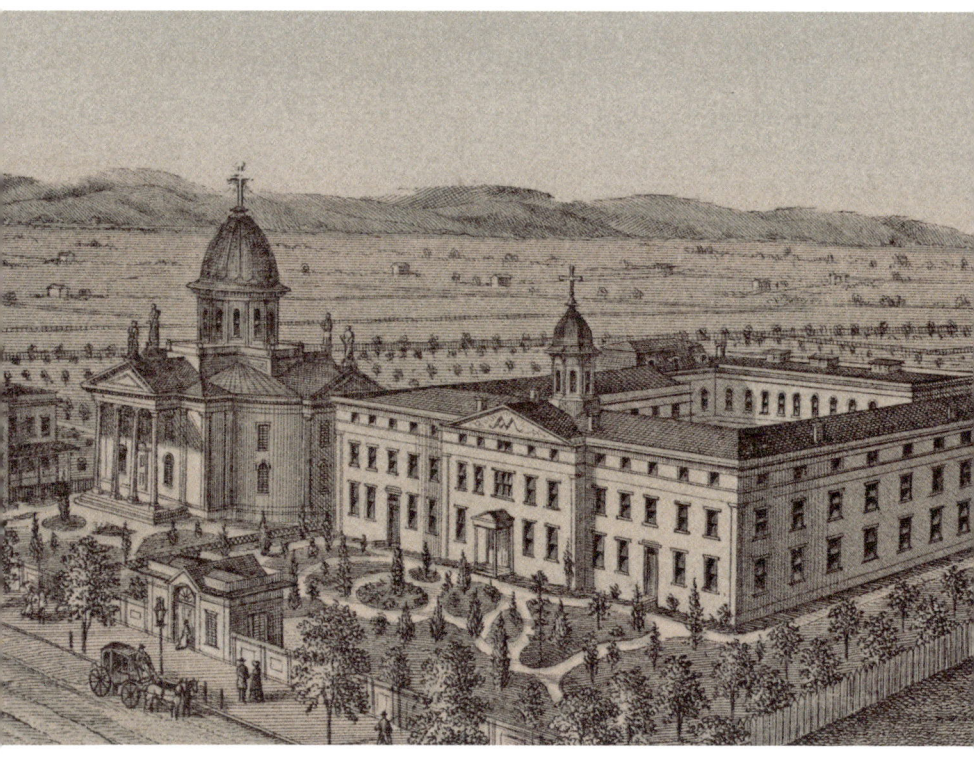

The Academy of Notre Dame was founded in 1851.

> "Everything seemed dark ... I had father, mother, brothers, and sisters; it seemed I would rather lose all of them than my poor grandpa. I was only a simple child, yet I knew what a great man he was."

Sarah hoped that attending the convent school, as her grandfather wished, would be a good experience for her. She and Elma traveled to San Jose, California, to enroll in the Academy of Notre Dame.

Sarah Winnemucca

Sarah loved her classes at the academy. The nuns at the convent taught history, geography, arithmetic, music, and writing, as well as embroidery and other forms of needlework. Sarah enjoyed needlework so much that she spent extra time on it. Sarah and Elma helped each other as they learned the routines of daily classes and homework. They also learned how to behave appropriately in society, which served Sarah well during her later life.

But sadly, Sarah and Elma's time at the convent school didn't last long. Most of the students at the school came from wealthy families. Their parents considered Indians to be savages and didn't want them near their daughters. These parents soon forced the nuns to send the Paiute girls away. Sarah didn't want to leave the convent school, but she had no choice. She would have to find a different path in life.

Sarah Winnemucca worked hard to create understanding.

Chapter Four
PRINCESS SARAH

When Sarah and Elma returned to Nevada, they tried to settle back into life among the Paiute.

Sarah was now 16 years old and considered old enough to get married. Some accounts say she married Mr. Snyder, her grandfather's "white brother," whom people also called the "white Winnemucca." Little is known about this man, including his first name, but he may have been a German immigrant who lived among the Paiute for many years. After 1861, marriages between American Indians and whites were against Nevada

Inspiring Stories

state law. If Snyder and Sarah were married, it was likely in a simple Paiute ceremony. Sarah herself never mentioned an early marriage in any of her writings. But one account said Snyder died during a visit to his family in Germany, so Sarah may have been a young widow.

Sarah was again living with her parents and siblings by 1864, when she was 20. Even though Sarah could read and write, few jobs were open to her. To earn money, she sometimes cooked, cleaned, or sewed for white people. Her love of needlework probably made this last task her favorite. Yet no Paiute could earn enough money to live comfortably. Railroads were now being built in Paiute territory. Railroad workers chopped down trees and disturbed the animals, just as the miners had done. Settlers continued to build homes and graze cattle on Paiute land. Many of Sarah's people were hungry and cold.

By September 1864 Winnemucca decided he needed to do something to help his family and the rest of his people. He, Sarah, and two of her siblings rode into

The population of Virginia City topped 25,000 during its heyday in the mid-1800s.

Virginia City to ask the people there for help. In Paiute society, this was a respectable thing to do. Paiutes were expected and honored to share what they had with the less fortunate. The family stood on a downtown street as Sarah translated Winnemucca's words to the people gathered there. He said, "I came to ask white man to give us something, but I don't want white man to give unless he is entirely willing." At the end of his speech, Sarah collected $25 in donations from the crowd, and Winnemucca bowed to them in respect. At the time, $25 was a good sum of money, but it wasn't enough to help many Paiute people.

Sarah and her father came up with a new plan to help their people. The Winnemucca family would appear in stage performances in Virginia City and later in San Francisco. They acted out scenes of what their audience believed to be Indian life, although the performances were more about Indian stereotypes than actual Paiute ways. They included scenes of a war council, battles, and dancing. Winnemucca also spoke of the Paiutes' hunger and other needs. Sarah translated his words into English.

People in Virginia City flocked to see the Winnemucca family. Old Winnemucca was an impressive figure. His nose was pierced with a 4-inch-long (10-centimeter) piece of bone. Onstage, he

Sarah Winnemucca

Old Winnemucca wore an impressive uniform when he performed onstage.

wore a coat with military braiding and brass epaulets. Sarah dressed as an Indian princess—although her buckskin dress was more something that a Plains Indian would wear than a traditional Paiute dress.

Inspiring Stories

Newspapers in Virginia City contained some favorable reviews of the performances. But when the show traveled to the Metropolitan Theater in San Francisco in October, it didn't get such a positive reception.

Many newspaper reporters mocked what they called a savage "Royal Family." While they admitted that Sarah had a "sweet English voice," they made fun of Winnemucca, saying that the Paiute language he spoke sounded like gibberish. Such articles didn't take the Paiutes or their needs seriously. The lack of concern was common then.

But one woman wrote a letter to the editor of a local newspaper. She said she was shocked that this respected native leader had to put on "degrading exhibitions" to help his family and other Paiutes. She urged the "People of California! People of Nevada … to rescue the Chief, his daughters … and provide for their immediate wants." She also encouraged them to send food and supplies to the Paiute people. But most white people didn't agree with her.

Sarah Winnemucca

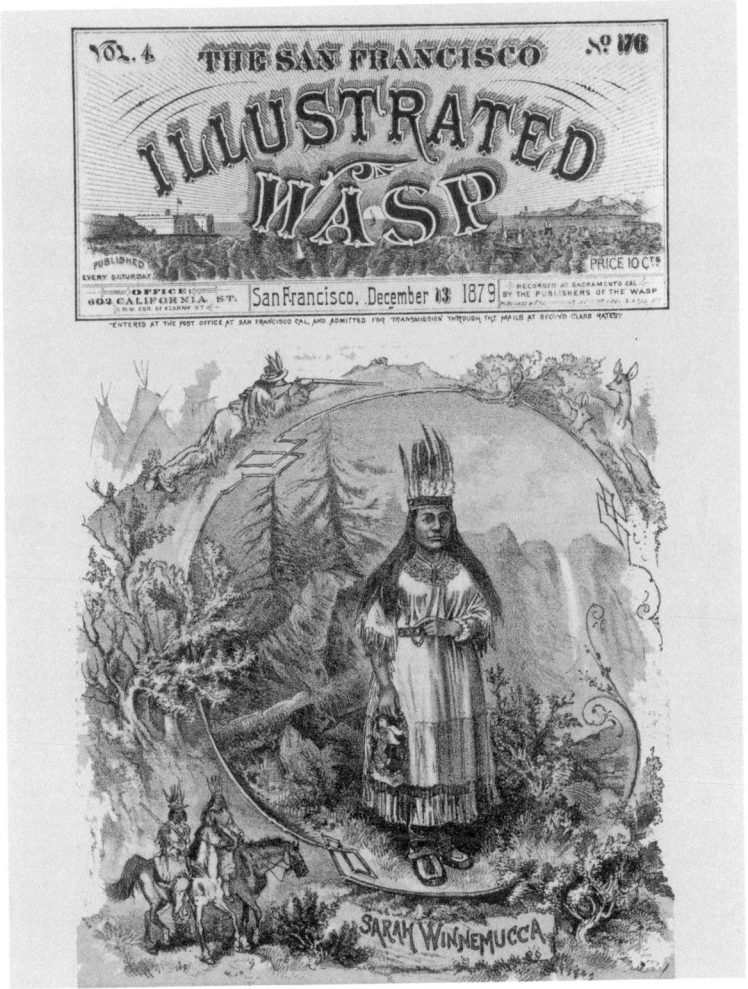

Sarah appeared on the cover of a San Francisco weekly magazine in 1879.

The shows weren't as successful as Sarah and her father had hoped. After paying theater rental and travel costs, Winnemucca had only enough money left to buy a few blankets and bags of flour for his people.

Inspiring Stories

Paiute performances in Virginia City (above) were better received than in California.

This wasn't enough to help the desperate Paiutes. Some started stealing settlers' cattle for food. Indians were also accused in the murder of two white men found near the Walker River. These acts increased the settlers' anger toward the Paiutes. It was a situation about to explode in violence.

In March 1865 some of Sarah's family members were camped near Mud Lake. Soldiers searching for cattle thieves entered the camp. At the time Sarah's father and almost all of the other men had left the camp to hunt. The soldiers killed 29 women, children, and elderly people. Sarah was staying at a camp in Dayton, Nevada, but learned the details of the massacre from her sister Mary, who was the only survivor. Sarah later wrote that the soldiers took "babies still tied in their baskets ... and threw them into the flames to see them burn alive." One of the children killed was Sarah's infant half-brother, the son of one of Winnemucca's other wives, who also died. Both Mary and Tuboitonie died a short time later, but it's not known if their deaths were related to the massacre.

Settlers were afraid that the Paiutes would seek revenge for the massacre. They urged the army to attack the Paiutes first, which it did. The Indians fought bravely and won some battles, but the army's far greater numbers assured that they would eventually win the war.

Noted photographer Timothy O'Sullivan photographed Pyramid Lake in 1867.

Chapter Five
FIGHTING FOR HER PEOPLE

Sarah was living on the Pyramid Lake Reservation with her brother Natchez and his wife by 1866. The reservation was established in 1864, and in the short time it had existed, several government agents had been in charge. One of the first agents, Warren Wasson, was honest and kind. He had given the Paiutes all the government supplies that had been delivered for them. He had helped in times of sickness or trouble.

But the men who replaced Wasson were different. They took the supplies meant for the Indians and kept or sold them. No family got everything they

Inspiring Stories

needed to survive. Sarah wrote, "A family numbering eight persons got two blankets, three shirts, no dress-goods. Some got a fish-hook and line; some got one and a half yards of flannel. ... It was the saddest affair I ever saw."

By 1868 an agent named Hugh Nugent was in charge of the reservation. He sold gunpowder to a young Paiute man, which was against reservation rules. The Paiute man was then killed for having the gunpowder. His family wanted to kill Nugent for causing the young man's death. Sarah and her brother knew that if Nugent was killed, white settlers would be furious and the Paiutes would be in danger.

Sarah and Natchez went to Nugent and tried to warn him, but he wouldn't listen to them. Natchez then learned that Paiutes coming to kill Nugent had instead killed two white men about 30 miles (48 km) from the reservation and stolen their horses. Natchez took a group of 30 Paiutes to try to find the killers.

Army Captain Aaron Jerome was stationed at nearby Fort Churchill. When he learned of the

WALKING IN TWO WORLDS

Sarah felt as if she lived in two worlds—the world of white people and the world of her Paiute people. It often wasn't easy to move between the two worlds. Many white people thought she was an uncivilized woman who drank alcohol and behaved inappropriately with men. On the other hand, many Indians weren't happy that she spoke English and associated with whites. They didn't like it that she often dressed in the clothing worn by fashionable white women at the time, including velvet dresses, gloves, and elegant hats. At Camp McDermit, she often rode a horse around the grounds dressed in her best clothes. She rode sidesaddle—the ladylike style used most often by wealthy white women.

Sarah often became upset when people on both sides criticized her and her behavior. Sarah won a hair-pulling fight in 1872 with a Paiute woman who spoke badly about Sarah's character. Sarah knocked her to the ground and said, "There, talk so about me to white folks, will you!" Just a few weeks later, Sarah got into a physical fight with a hotel waiter after he insulted her. Sarah ended up with a split lip and the waiter with a black eye.

Sarah wanted the best for her people, but wasn't sure that she wanted to live like them. Sarah spoke to a Nevada newspaper reporter in 1870. After discussing the needs of the Paiutes, Sarah said, "I like this Indian life tolerably well; however, my only object in staying with these people is that I may do them good. I would rather be with my people, but not to live with them as they live. ... My happiest life has been ... living among the whites."

Inspiring Stories

situation, he had a message delivered to Sarah. He asked her and Natchez to meet him that night to tell him their side of the story before the army took any action against the Indians.

Sarah was desperate. Natchez had left very early that day, and Sarah didn't know when he would return. She decided to try to write to Captain Jerome. After all, her grandfather Truckee's "rag friend" had often helped keep him safe. But neither she nor anyone else on the reservation had paper, pen, or ink.

Sarah solved this problem by asking for a stick with a sharp point and fish blood. Using these unusual tools, she carefully scratched a reply onto the letter the captain had sent. It said:

> "Hon[orable] Sir: My brother is not here. I am looking for him every minute. We will go as soon as he comes in. If he comes in to-night, we will come some time during the night. Yours, S.W."

Sarah's quick thinking paid off. Captain Jerome waited until she and Natchez could tell him the Paiutes' side of the story. Jerome spoke to his

Camp McDermit was in northern Nevada.

commanding officer, Captain Dudley Seward, about problems at the reservation. Captain Seward then invited the Paiutes to live at Camp McDermit. This army outpost, later called Fort McDermit, was 300 miles (483 km) northwest of Pyramid Lake, close to the Oregon border.

Sarah traveled extensively but lived most of her life in Nevada.

Sarah wasn't sure leaving the reservation and traveling the distance to the army camp was a good idea. Some of the other tribe members agreed with her. Natchez convinced them that the difficult journey was a risk worth taking. He hoped that the Paiute would find a better life at the camp, saying, "Because white people [here] are bad that is no reason why the soldiers should be bad, too."

Sarah Winnemucca

Many Pyramid Lake Paiutes set out on the 28-day trip. At Camp McDermit they discovered that Captain Seward was a man of his word. The Paiutes had plenty of supplies and were no longer hungry and cold. Natchez convinced Old Winnemucca and the people who were living with him in the mountains to also come to the camp. By the end of the year, about 900 Paiutes received shelter at the camp. They would spend several good years there.

A Northern Paiute woman ground seeds in the doorway of a dwelling.

# Chapter Six
A STRUGGLE TO SURVIVE

Sarah mostly enjoyed her years at Camp McDermit. In addition to working as an interpreter, she also worked as the caretaker of the camp hospital for a time. In 1870 she met a young soldier, Edward Bartlett. He was charming and handsome and appreciated Sarah's beauty and intelligence. Sarah fell in love with Bartlett. What she didn't realize was that he had many problems. His wealthy family had already saved him from prison for stealing from the army. At Camp McDermit he was known to drink and gamble

Sarah lived in Salt Lake City for a short time.

too much. Sarah decided to marry him anyway. The couple traveled by train to Salt Lake City, Utah, and were married there January 29, 1871. They couldn't be married in Nevada because of the state law that made marriages between Indians and whites illegal.

After just three weeks of marriage, Sarah realized she had made a mistake. Still in Salt Lake City,

Sarah Winnemucca

Bartlett was drinking heavily and had taken some of Sarah's jewelry and pawned it for money to buy more alcohol. Natchez came to Salt Lake City to take Sarah home. Neither he nor Winnemucca had been pleased with Sarah's choice of a husband. Sarah went back to her jobs at the army camp, and Bartlett resigned from the army and returned to New York. Later that year he married a white woman, Louisa Butler, without bothering to get a divorce from Sarah. He may have considered his marriage to an Indian woman not legal.

Sarah's family had more troubles to deal with. Natchez was arrested in 1874 after arguing with Calvin Bateman, the agent at Pyramid Lake Reservation. Natchez was upset when Bateman refused to give government-issued blankets to Indians who didn't live on the reservation. Bateman had him arrested and sent to Alcatraz Prison in San Francisco on the charge of causing unrest on the reservation. Many white residents of the area spoke out in support of Natchez, though, and he was released after 11 days in jail.

Inspiring Stories

The next year, Sarah found herself in jail as well. In the rough railroad town of Winnemucca—named after Sarah's father—a white man named Julius Argasse tried to force his way into Sarah's home. Sarah fought back, using a penknife to cut his face. She was arrested and charged with assault with intent to do bodily harm. Many Paiutes feared that Sarah would never receive a fair hearing in the white courts. But a well-known white lawyer, Mac Bonnifield, volunteered to defend Sarah. He called many witnesses to speak about her good character and trustworthiness. Sarah was set free.

Later that year, Sarah moved again. She joined her father and his band at the Malheur Reservation in southeastern Oregon. Sarah got a job as an interpreter at the reservation.

The reservation's name, malheur, means "bad luck" in French. But at first, the Paiute found the reservation to be a good place. The agent, Samuel Parrish, was an honest, fair man. He distributed all government supplies and helped the Paiutes dig an irrigation ditch, plant crops, and build a schoolhouse, blacksmith shop, and carpenter shop. At the new schoolhouse, Sarah helped Parrish's sister-in-law, Annie Parrish, teach English to the Paiute children. Annie also helped the girls at the school make dresses for themselves. The Paiute called Annie their "white lily mother." After hearing

Samuel Parrish treated the Paiutes well.

about the good conditions at the reservation, other Paiutes moved there. By the end of 1875, nearly 750 Paiutes lived at Malheur. But as always, the good times didn't last.

In 1876 some of the neighboring white settlers began to complain that Parrish was giving the

Malheur Indians too many supplies and overpaying those who held jobs at the reservation. At the same time, the Bureau of Indian Affairs changed its staff. Many members of religious organizations replaced existing Indian agents on reservations.

President Ulysses S. Grant appointed William Rinehart to replace Parrish as the Malheur agent. Sarah and the rest of the Paiute were very upset. Winnemucca told Parrish, "I do not want anyone but you. I am going to see the soldier-father tomorrow. I know they will keep you here for me, or I think they can if they wish to."

Winnemucca and several other Indian leaders went to Camp Harney and talked to the commanding officer, Major John Green. He listened to what they had to say and even wrote a letter to Washington on their behalf, but it did no good. Rinehart arrived on June 28, and Parrish left the next day. Sarah and her family never saw him again.

Rinehart was the opposite of Parrish. He expected complete obedience from the Paiute people. One day

Sarah Winnemucca

Willliam Rinehart thought of American Indians as the enemy.

he thought that a little boy was laughing at something he said. Sarah said he picked up the boy by the ear, threw him against a wall, and then kicked him. Sarah tried to explain to Rinehart that the boy didn't understand English and couldn't have been laughing at him, but he didn't believe her. He also didn't

Inspiring Stories

A Paiute encampment had traditional dwellings and canvas tents.

distribute the supplies fairly. He said that each man, woman, and boy on the reservation would receive a dollar each day for the work that they did. But instead of paying them in cash, he put dollar amounts on clothing and blankets and used these items as payment for their work—items that they were entitled to in the first place. He also withheld food and closed the reservation school.

Some Paiutes, including Winnemucca, left the reservation for the nearby mountains. But Sarah didn't join them, even though Rinehart had fired her from her job after she complained about his treatment of the people. That summer she had met and fallen in love with a man named Joseph Satwaller. Sarah received a divorce in September from Edward Bartlett and took back her last name of Winnemucca.

On November 13, 1876, 32-year-old Sarah married Satwaller in the home of her friends Charles and Annie Parrish in Canyon City. After the wedding, Sarah and her new husband left Malheur, possibly to live at the Warm Springs reservation. Little more is known about Satwaller, since Sarah never mentioned him in her later writings about her life. They separated sometime before the spring of 1878, and Sarah's life again took a new turn.

A Paiute woman held her child, who was nestled in a traditional cradleboard.

Chapter Seven
BANNOCK WAR

After her marriage broke up, Sarah was working for a woman near Prairie City, Oregon. In April and May 1878, men from Malheur reservation twice visited her at the woman's house. They told Sarah that the conditions at the reservation had grown worse and that even more people were hungry. They begged her to go to Camp Harney and ask the army officers there for help. Sarah wasn't sure that the officers would listen to her, but she agreed to go to Malheur.

When Sarah reached the reservation, she found that Agent Rinehart wasn't distributing the food and clothing that the people were supposed to receive. Many people were going hungry, and to make matters worse, Sarah's father and brother weren't there. They had gone to talk to the Bannock people, who were planning to go to war against the whites.

The Bannock were from southern Idaho. The tribe of 1,000 people spoke the same language as the Northern Paiute, but they were known for being more aggressive. They hunted buffalo, rather than rabbits. But their troubles were similar to those of the Paiutes. Whites had killed off most buffalo. Settlers' livestock had destroyed the camas roots, another major food for the Bannocks. Greedy Indian agents had withheld promised supplies. The Bannocks were slowly starving. And then white men assaulted a girl of the tribe. The girl's brother killed another white man in retaliation. The situation was about to explode.

Sarah told the men at Malheur that she would travel to Washington, D.C., and talk to the U.S. president about the Paiutes' difficulties. She planned to take a wagon and two white passengers to Silver City,

Sarah Winnemucca

An illustration of a group of Bannock appeared in Harper's Weekly *in 1878.*

Idaho. Then she would travel to Elko, Nevada, where she would sell the wagon and board a train for the long trip to Washington.

But Sarah never made it to Washington. As they neared the Idaho border, a man warned her and her passengers that the Bannocks were at war and that no travel was safe. Sarah took her passengers to a nearby house, where she spoke to Army Captain Reuben

Bernard. He told her alarming news. Winnemucca, Natchez, and other Kuyuidika-a were trapped inside the main Bannock camp. Winnemucca had hoped to convince the Bannocks that it was in their own best interest not to fight. They couldn't leave the camp without seeming to betray the Bannocks, whose war chiefs hoped to convince the Paiutes to be their allies. Winnemucca also worried that whites might believe that his band had indeed joined the Bannocks.

Bernard asked his commanding officer, General Oliver Howard, to allow Sarah to be an interpreter and scout for the army. Howard agreed and said the army would welcome the Kuyuidika-a back once they returned. Sarah needed to get to Winnemucca and Natchez with this news. Accompanied only by two Paiute men, she set off on the dangerous and exhausting mission of traveling 220 miles (354 km) by horse to rescue her trapped people. If she was successful, the army would pay her $500.

Sarah and the men rode almost nonstop for three days and nights. She later wrote that "[t]his was the

A drawing of Sarah on an Army mission appeared in a 1906 Oregon newspaper.

hardest work I ever did for the government in all my life." When Sarah and her companions neared the Bannock camp, they discovered how difficult their mission was going to be. There were more than 325 lodges and 450 Bannock warriors surrounding the Paiutes. Sarah thought quickly. She changed from her dress into traditional Paiute clothing. She loosened her curled hair, dabbed paint on her face, and wrapped herself in a blanket.

Inspiring Stories

Oliver Howard was known as the "praying general" for his strong moral beliefs.

Sarah sneaked into the camp, found Winnemucca, and told him about General Howard's plan. She helped Winnemucca plan how the Paiutes would escape while pretending to go about their daily routines. The next day, their plan succeeded. Several years later, she wrote, "I, only an Indian woman, went and saved my father and his people." Winnemucca was pleased with his daughter, telling his people later that "hereafter we will look upon her as our chieftain, for none of us are worthy of being chief but her."

Unfortunately, Sarah's heroic actions didn't solve her people's problems. The army defeated the Bannocks by the end of the year. The government then ordered all Indians involved in the Bannock War to be sent to the Yakima Reservation in the state of Washington. That included the Paiutes, even though only a few Paiutes had fought alongside the Bannocks.

Sarah was horrified. The order was not only unfair but also a death sentence for some Paiutes. It was the middle of winter, and they had to travel 350 miles (563 km) north through snow-covered mountains. She wondered about the nature of a U.S. president who would condemn innocent people to die. She questioned "whether he is made of wood or rock, for ... [n]o human being would do such a thing as that."

Sarah couldn't convince the army officers to ignore the government orders. She accompanied her people on their bitter journey. Babies, new mothers,

American Indians lost most of their land and were forced to live on reservations.

and old people died during the month-long march. Things didn't improve once the Paiute reached the Yakima reservation, either. The Yakima people were traditional enemies of the Paiutes and weren't happy to share their reservation with them. The Indian agent, James Wilbur, didn't even know the Paiutes were coming. He reluctantly ordered a shed built for them. Sarah and the rest of the Paiutes huddled together in the unheated shelter to stay warm.

When spring came, the surviving Paiutes learned that Wilbur was much like Rinehart, the agent at Malheur. Wilbur was a Methodist minister and insisted that the Indians convert to Christianity before they received any supplies. He didn't even allow the Paiutes to keep the wheat they grew that year. Instead, he gave it to the Yakima converts. Sarah later angrily told him "hell is full of just such Christians as you are."

Sarah had been ready to go to Washington to talk to the president before. Now she knew that she had to go. If she could explain the Paiutes' needs to the president, perhaps they could return to their own territory.

But first, she decided to give a series of lectures in San Francisco about the Paiutes' problems. Sarah hoped to gain support from these appearances. She also wanted to be able to express herself clearly and strongly when she finally met the president.

Sarah (from left), Old Winnemucca, Natchez, and Captain Jim traveled to Washington, D.C.

Chapter Eight
LECTURER AND AUTHOR

Sarah's successful lectures in San Francisco boosted her confidence. She felt ready to talk to President Rutherford B. Hayes about the Paiutes' troubles.

Sarah, Winnemucca, Natchez, and Captain Jim, another Paiute leader, took the train to Washington, D.C., in January 1880. The transcontinental railroad allowed them to reach the nation's capital in a week. A Bureau of Indian Affairs official met and escorted them during their stay.

Inspiring Stories

On her second day in Washington, Sarah met with Secretary of the Interior Carl Schurz. She translated Winnemucca's and Natchez's words, and Schurz seemed to sympathize with their concerns. He even agreed to write a letter supporting the Paiutes' return to their Great Basin homeland and promised to provide them with 100 canvas tents for shelter.

Sarah was pleased with Schurz's reaction, but her meeting with the president was a disappointment. President Hayes paused only for a minute as he passed Sarah in a White House waiting room. He shook her hand and asked, "Did you get all you want for your people?" Sarah replied, "Yes, sir, as far as I know." Hayes responded, "That is well" before he quickly left the room. Sarah, who had hoped Hayes would be more interested in her people's plight, felt the meeting she had spent so much time planning and preparing for had been a failure.

When Sarah and her family returned to Yakima, they eagerly waited for the supplies and tents Schurz had promised, but they never arrived. Sarah also asked

SARAH'S FIRST LECTURES

Before she went to Washington, D.C., Sarah delivered a series of lectures at elegant halls and theaters in San Francisco in November and December 1879. Her audience was made up of wealthy, well-educated white people. Sarah knew she needed their support for her cause to succeed.

Many had never seen an American Indian before. When Sarah walked onstage, a reporter said she "wore a short buckskin dress, the skirt bordered with fringe and embroidery, short sleeves, disclosing beautifully-rounded brown arms, and scarlet leggin[g]s, with trimmings of fringe. On her head she wore a proud head dress of eagle's feathers, set in a scarlet crown, contrasting well with her flowing black locks."

The audience was amazed by Sarah's appearance, but even more so by her speech. The reporter remarked on Sarah's "flow of ... natural ... language ... [and] easy, unembarrassed manner" as she spoke of her life and her people. Her talk combined stories, sarcasm, impressions, and dramatic gestures. Again and again, the audience burst into "laughter and rounds of applause."

Sarah said in one lecture, "I am appealing to you to help my people, to send teachers and books among us. Educate us. ... I call upon white people in their private houses. They will not touch my fingers for fear of getting soiled." She noted sarcastically, "That is the Christianity of white people." Sarah went on to say: "The proverb says the big fish eat up the little fishes and we Indians are the little fish and you eat us all up and drive us from home. Where can we poor Indians go if the government will not help us? If your people will help us, and you have good hearts ... I will promise to educate my people and make them law-abiding citizens. ... It can be done—it can be done."

Agent Wilbur when the Paiutes might leave for their traditional home, but he said he hadn't received any official notice from the government and wouldn't take the letter Schurz had given Sarah as proof. Upset, Sarah sent a telegram to Schurz asking about the food and supplies. Schurz responded by saying that the Paiute should go to the Malheur reservation. Sarah knew that the hungry people couldn't travel 300 miles (483 km) in the winter cold and snow to Malheur.

At first the Paiutes were angry with the government and Wilbur. Then some of them thought that Sarah might have lied to them or even taken money to betray them. Sarah was deeply hurt and tried to explain the situation to them. "I know I have told you more lies than I have hair on my head. I tell you ... they were the words of the white people, not mine."

Unwelcome at Yakima, Sarah needed a place to live. She wrote to General Howard, who was stationed 60 miles (97 km) from Yakima at the Vancouver Barracks. The Indians taken prisoner after the Bannock War were being held there. Howard hired

Sarah Winnemucca

Sarah posed for a studio photograph in 1880.

Sarah to work as an interpreter and teacher at the barracks. Among the 53 prisoners were 18 children, whom Sarah taught to read and write. Howard was pleased with Sarah's work at the barracks and even wrote an official letter of recommendation for her.

Sarah's work at the prison camp gave her an unexpected opportunity to again meet U.S. President Rutherford Hayes. He and his wife were touring the

Inspiring Stories

camp and visited Sarah's classroom. This time, Sarah was determined that the president would listen to her. She asked that the Paiute people be reunited in one place where they could live permanently. "You are a husband and father, and you know how you would suffer to be separated from your wife and children by force, as my people still are, husbands from wives, parents from children, notwithstanding Secretary Schurz's order," she told Hayes. The president listened to her and said he would do what he could. Yet once again, nothing changed for Sarah and her people.

In 1881 Sarah finally received the $500 for her scout work during the Bannock War. She used some of the money to travel to Henry's Lake, Montana—now in Idaho—to visit her sister. Elma lived there with her husband, John Smith, a lumberjack. Sarah was happy to see her sister for the first time in many years. The sisters traveled together by train to Winnemucca to visit their family there. During her time with Elma, she may have met Lewis Hopkins, who would become her next husband. At 32, Hopkins was a handsome

Sarah Winnemucca

Sarah's sister, Elma Smith, in 1919, the year before she died

man five years younger than Sarah. He had served as a lieutenant in the army, so some people believe Sarah and he may have first met during the Bannock War. The two married in December 1881 in San Francisco.

But Sarah had made another bad choice. Sarah had hoped to start another lecture tour, this time in the northeastern United States. She would speak to people there about the Paiutes' need for land, food, and legal rights. But Hopkins quickly gambled away $500 of Sarah's savings. The couple moved to Pyramid Lake Reservation, where they stayed several months with Sarah's brother Tom. They later stayed with Elma and her husband before finally reaching Boston, Massachusetts, in the spring of 1883.

During the time Sarah and Hopkins were in Idaho, her father was dying in California. Winnemucca had traveled with Sarah's brother Lee and other family members to visit a friend when he fell ill. He died October 21, 1882. Sarah was sad that she hadn't been able to be with her father at the end. She decided that her lecture tour would honor Winnemucca's memory by trying to get the help for his people that he worked for all his life.

Sarah and her husband stayed with sisters Elizabeth Peabody and Mary Peabody Mann in Boston. The

Sarah Winnemucca

two elderly sisters may have helped set up the lecture tour. Sarah gave more than 300 lectures to large church groups and other gatherings in New York, Connecticut, Rhode Island, Maryland, Massachusetts, and Pennsylvania. People were more than willing to pay the 10- to 25-cent admission charge to hear her speak. Sarah

Sarah's husband, Lewis Hopkins

and her husband used the fees to help pay their living expenses. Lewis Hopkins often appeared onstage to introduce his wife. When she spoke, Sarah wore a buckskin dress, leather leggings, and moccasins. This clothing wasn't traditional for the Paiutes, but instead was commonly worn by Indian women of the Great Plains tribes. Sarah may have chosen the outfit because her audience was more familiar with the people and dress of those tribes. Sometimes she wore a small gold crown and carried an embroidered bag.

As she traveled, Sarah asked people to sign a petition asking that Indians receive land of their own and also be treated as U.S. citizens. More than 5,000 people signed her petition.

Women at Sarah's lectures were eager to hear about Paiute family life. When Mary Peabody Mann suggested that Sarah write a book, Sarah realized it would be a great way to spread her message to even more people. Mary offered to correct spelling errors and arrange for publication. Lewis researched facts in libraries. Sarah poured her heart and soul into her book. She wrote directly to those who had hurt her people but still had the power to help them. She begged, saying: "Oh, for shame! ... [Y]ou, who call yourselves the great civilization; you ... who have [pledged] with God to make this land the home of the free and the brave. ... I am crying out to you for

Sarah Winnemucca

PETITION
To the Honorable Congress of the United States.

Whereas, the tribe of Piute Indians that formerly occupied the greater part of Nevada and now diminished by its sufferings and wrongs to one-third of its original number, has always kept its promise of peace and friendliness to the whites since they first entered their country, and has of late been deprived of the Malheur Reservation decreed to them by President Grant:

I, Sarah Winnemucca Hopkins, granddaughter of Captain Truckee, who promised friendship for his tribe to General Fremont, whom he guided into California and served through the Mexican war — together with the undersigned friends who sympathize in the cause of my people — do petition the Honorable Congress of the United States to restore to them said Malheur Reservation, which is well watered and timbered, and large enough to afford homes and support for them all, where they can enjoy lands in severalty without loosing their tribal relations, so essential to their happiness and good character, and where their citizenship, implied in this distribution of land, will defend them from the encroachments of the white settlers, so detrimental to their interest and their virtues. And especially do we petition for the return of that portion of the tribe arbitrarily removed from the Malheur Reservation, after the Bannock war, to the Yakima Reservation, on Columbia River in which removal families were ruthlessly separated, and have never ceased to pine for husbands, wives, and children, which restoration was pledged to them by the Secretary of the Interior in 1880, but has not been fulfilled.

Boston Dec. 1883

Sarah circulated petitions in support of the Paiutes, often spelled Piutes at that time.

justice—yes, pleading for the far-off plains of the West for … my people."

Sarah's book, *Life Among the Piutes: Their Wrongs and Claims*, was published late in 1883. The eight-chapter, leather-bound book sold for $1. It included many letters from Nevada citizens and army officers who praised Sarah's good character. Mary and Sarah hoped the letters would help offset the negative things some people were saying about Sarah. People such as William Rinehart resented Sarah's criticism of Indian agents and the reservation system. They hoped people would stop listening to Sarah if they believed she was dishonest.

The book was a success, although Sarah sometimes gave wrong dates for past events and told some events in the wrong order. But she also included word-for-word whole speeches and conversations held long ago. People have questioned whether her account was accurate. But according to historians, using exact dates wasn't a Paiute tradition. The Paiutes also memorized and spoke all their history and stories instead of writing them down. Sarah's background as the daughter and granddaughter of tribal leaders makes her detailed recollection of speeches and conversations believable.

After her successful lecture tour and book, Sarah probably hoped that life would become easier and

LIFE AMONG THE PIUTES:

Their Wrongs and Claims.

BY

SARAH WINNEMUCCA HOPKINS.

EDITED BY

MRS. HORACE MANN,

AND

PRINTED FOR THE AUTHOR.

BOSTON:
FOR SALE BY CUPPLES, UPHAM & CO.
283 WASHINGTON STREET;
G. P. PUTNAM'S SONS, NEW YORK;
AND BY THE AUTHOR.
1883.

Sarah's book was edited by Mary Peabody Mann, the widow of Horace Mann. He was an educator who advanced the cause of free public schools.

simpler. But Sarah's life, which had been so eventful, wasn't about to settle down.

A statue of Sarah sat outside the U.S. Capitol before taking its place in Statuary Hall.

Chapter Nine
LATER YEARS

Sarah continued her lecture tour in early 1884 in Baltimore, Maryland. She gave more than 60 lectures in the city. Sarah's petition was presented to the U.S. Congress in the spring, and she testified before the Senate subcommittee on Indian affairs. She asked that Camp McDermit be turned into a Paiute reservation, with land given to each family to farm. But her efforts were unsuccessful. The Department of War wanted the army camp to remain under its control. Congress instead voted that the Paiute could return to the Pyramid Lake reservation, where each family

Inspiring Stories

FOREIGNERS IN THEIR OWN LAND

During Sarah's lifetime, American Indians weren't U.S. citizens. They didn't have the rights that the U.S. Constitution guarantees and that laws protect. Unlike immigrants from other countries, there was no official way that American Indians could become citizens. In her book, Sarah wrote about the different treatment of immigrants and native people. It wasn't until 1924 that Congress passed a law making all American Indians U.S. citizens. Since Sarah died in 1891, she was never a citizen. Officially, she was a foreigner in the land where she was born—the land her people had lived in long before white people arrived.

was to receive 160 acres (65 hectares) of land. But white settlers had claimed almost all of the good farmland in the area. The Paiute would have a hard time making a living at Pyramid Lake.

Saddened, Sarah returned to Nevada in August. Her husband, who was sick with tuberculosis, remained in the East. Despite the success of Sarah's lectures and books, she had little money. Lewis had spent some of their money on alcohol and gambling, and another portion had gone for his medical care.

Sarah Winnemucca

On her way home, Sarah gave nearly $200 to her brother Natchez to settle a debt. When she reached Winnemucca, she had only $50 to her name.

Sarah knew she would have to get a job. But Indian agents refused to hire her as a reservation interpreter or teacher because she had criticized them. When Sarah tried to earn money by lecturing in Reno and Carson City, few people came. Sarah began to question if her book and lectures had accomplished anything positive.

Sarah's brother, Natchez

Sarah was sad for another reason. Many Paiutes continued to distrust her. Even though Sarah now needed money, they knew she had lived well in the past while the Paiutes had suffered. After a year of these struggles, Sarah told a local newspaper reporter that she was abandoning "the fight. … I have worked for freedom. I have labored to give my race a voice in the affairs of the nation, but they prefer to be slaves so let it be."

Yet Sarah overcame her grief and doubts to rise to a new challenge. In the spring of 1885, she moved to Natchez's ranch near Lovelock, Nevada. In that tiny community, Sarah began an unusual school.

At the time the government ran "Indian schools" around the country. At the schools, which were usually far away from their homes, Indian students were supposed to learn white ways of life. They were often given American names and were punished for speaking their native languages or practicing native customs.

Sarah's school, which she named the Peabody Indian School after Elizabeth Peabody, was different. She wanted her people to learn English, but she also wanted them to keep their own identity. As she explained in a letter to the Paiutes in California, her education plan would "fit your little ones for the battle of life, so that they can attend to their own affairs instead of having to call in a white man [for help]."

THE PEABODY SISTERS

Elizabeth Peabody and her sister Mary Peabody Mann were well-known social reformers in Massachusetts. Both sisters were in their 70s by the time they became acquainted with Sarah Winnemucca. The three women quickly became close friends.

Elizabeth, who never married, was a teacher and writer who opened the first English-language kindergarten in the United States. The idea of schools for young children that emphasized learning through play began in Germany. Elizabeth spread the idea to the United States. She was also a writer and bookstore owner. She died in 1894.

Elizabeth Peabody

Mary Peabody Mann was also a teacher and writer. Her husband was the famous educator Horace Mann. She published a children's book and also opened her own school in Salem, Massachusetts. A novel, written when she was 80, was published after her death in 1887.

Inspiring Stories

Sarah sometimes wore a black velvet costume during her lectures about the Paiutes.

Sarah was a gifted teacher. Her students enjoyed learning so much that they playfully scribbled English words on fences around town. Elizabeth Peabody's

Sarah Winnemucca

friend Alice Chapin, who came from the East to teach at the school for a time, said that many of the students had learned more than white children of the same age. Peabody and others sent money to help support the school. Yet the school's success wasn't enough to keep it going.

Reservation officials pressured Paiute parents to send their children to the government schools. Sometimes the officials took the children away by force. Money was also a problem. Some supporters of the school had doubts about how Sarah was using the funds they sent. When Sarah traveled to the eastern United States in 1887 to raise money for the school, she reconciled with Lewis Hopkins. He returned to Nevada with her, and Sarah's friends worried that he would spend money meant for the school on drinking and gambling.

Sarah's friends were right. After Natchez raised a good crop of wheat meant to support the school, Lewis sold the wheat and took most of the money for himself. He then went to San Francisco. Sarah sided with Lewis, which upset Natchez. Lewis ran through the money in a few weeks before returning to the ranch, where he died on October 18. Even though Lewis had caused her so much trouble, Sarah grieved when he died.

Sarah also had health problems. She suffered with rheumatism and from what was probably malaria. She managed to keep the Peabody school open until 1889. At that time many Paiute parents decided their children didn't need to attend school. They believed in the growing Ghost Dance movement, which promised a future where Indians would return to their traditional ways and wouldn't need to know English. Later that year Sarah moved to Henry's Lake to live with her sister Elma. Sarah spent the rest of her life with Elma, whose husband had died earlier that year.

The Ghost Dance movement continued to spread. A Northern Paiute man named Wovoka advised hard work and nonviolence toward whites. He said performing the Ghost Dance would inspire the spirits to make white people disappear. Alarmed, soldiers attacked Ghost Dance followers at Wounded Knee Creek, South Dakota, in 1890. Nearly 300 Lakota,

Sarah Winnemucca

Members of the 7th Cavalry after the massacre at Wounded Knee

mostly women and children, were killed. After the massacre, Sarah urged the Paiutes who lived near her to remain calm. She helped prevent their anger from turning into further bloodshed.

Sarah died unexpectedly at age 47 on October 16, 1891. Sarah had been sick for several years, but the cause of her death is unknown. She was buried in an unmarked grave near her brother-in-law, John Smith.

Inspiring Stories

Her brother Natchez arrived too late for the burial. He died in 1907 at Pyramid Lake.

Though some of her efforts failed, Sarah Winnemucca achieved many things for herself and her people. Some native people still have mixed feelings about her, but many respect her. In 1993 the Nevada Writers Hall of Fame included her among its members. In 1994 an elementary school in Reno, Nevada, was named for her. In 2005 a statue of Sarah was unveiled at the U.S. Capitol in Washington, D.C. A duplicate statue also stands in the Nevada capitol in Carson City. Sculptor Benjamin Victor showed Sarah holding a book, which represented her writing and her interest in education. She also holds a shell flower, which represents her Paiute name and her pride in her heritage.

Sarah Winnemucca was a strong woman who never stopped fighting for a better life for herself and her people. She remains an inspiration today.

Sarah Winnemucca

A bronze state of Sarah Winnemucca stands in the capitol in Carson City.

Timeline

1857
Lives with Major Ormsby's family in Genoa, Utah Territory, now Nevada, for a year

1844
Sarah Winnemucca is born in what is now western Nevada

1850
Travels to California with her grandfather, mother, and siblings

1860
Pyramid Lake War takes place; Captain Truckee dies; Sarah attends convent school in California

1871
Marries Edward Bartlett

1865–66
Lives at Pyramid Lake Reservation with brother Natchez

1864
Makes first stage appearances in Virginia City, Nevada, and San Francisco, California; reservations at Pyramid Lake and Walker River become official

1868–71
Works at Camp McDermit as an interpreter, scout, and hospital matron

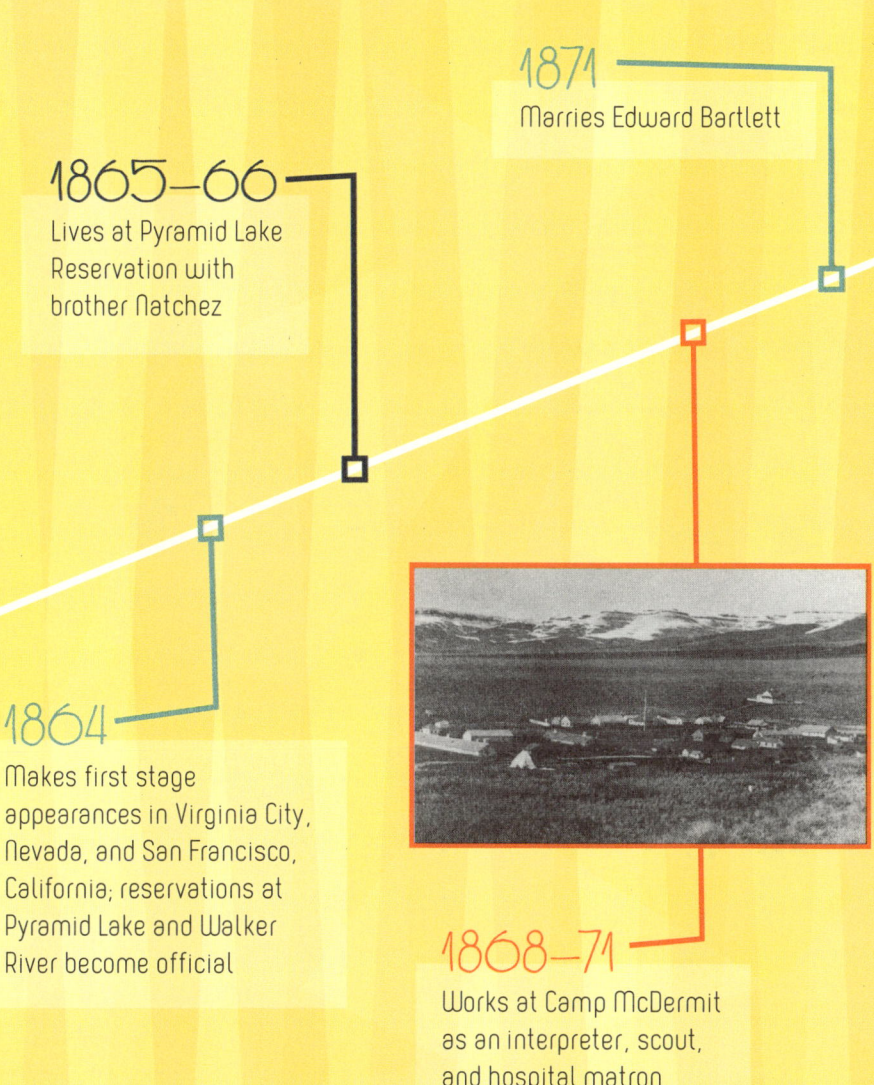

Timeline

1880
Travels to Washington, D.C., with her father and brother to ask for her people's release from the reservation

1879
Lectures in San Francisco to publicize her people's plight

1876
Works as an interpreter at Malheur reservation; marries Joseph Satwaller and leaves reservation

1881
Marries Lewis Hopkins

1878
Works for the Army during the Bannock War and moves to the Yakima reservation in Washington state

1889
Closes school and moves to Montana

1885
Starts Peabody Indian School in Lovelock, Nevada

1887
Lewis Hopkins dies

1883
Begins tour of the eastern United States and gives more than 300 lectures; her autobiography, *Life Among the Piutes: Their Wrongs and Claims*, is published

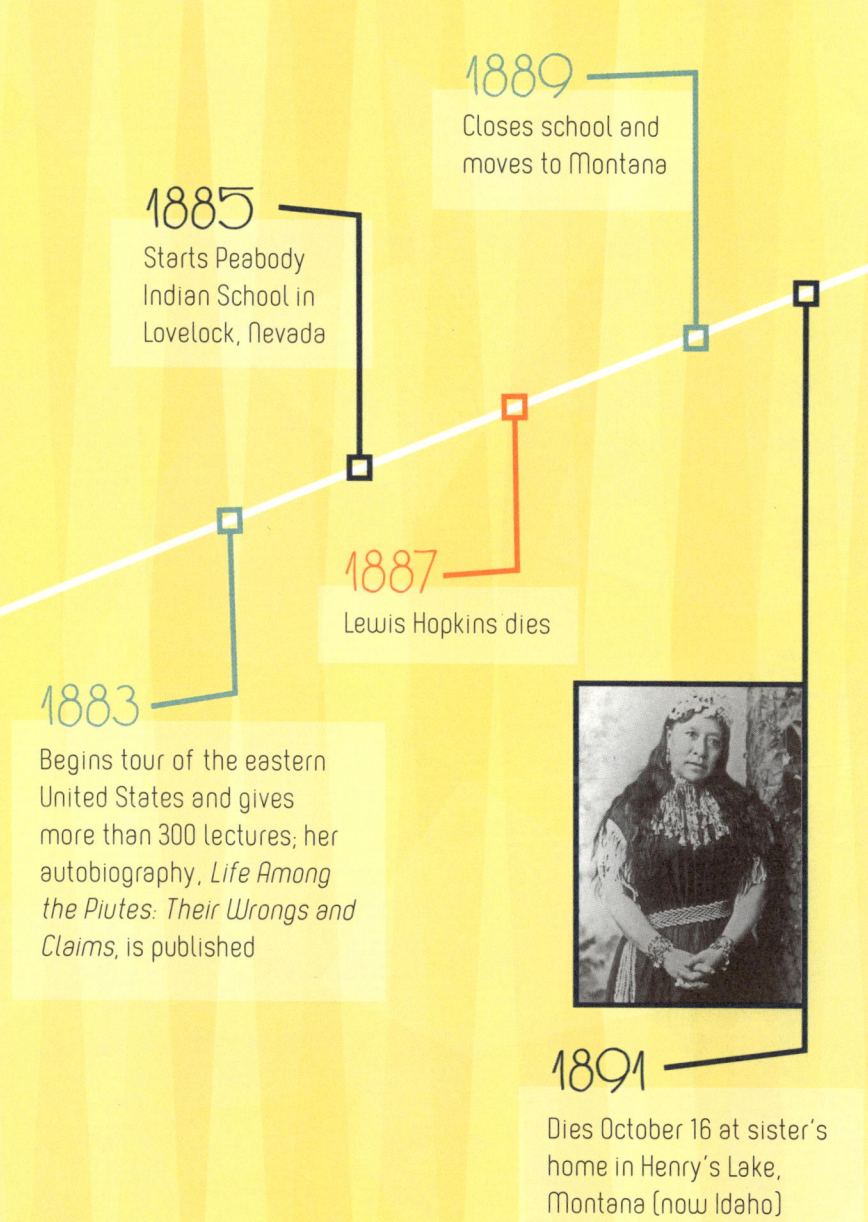

1891
Dies October 16 at sister's home in Henry's Lake, Montana (now Idaho)

Glossary

convent—building where a group of religious women live

degrading—something that makes people feel useless or bad

eloquent—ability to speak in a powerful and convincing way

interpreter—person who hears one language and translates its meaning to another

lode—large underground deposit of a metal or mineral

massacre—the deliberate killing of a group of unarmed people

petition—letter signed by many people asking leaders for a change

reservation—area of land set aside by the U.S. government for American Indians; in Canada reservations are called reserves

retaliate—to strike back in response to another attack

sarcasm—humor that points out someone's mistakes or weaknesses

OTHER BOOKS IN THIS SERIES

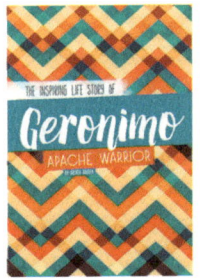
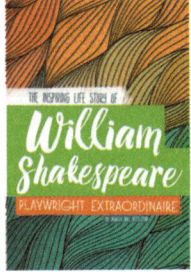

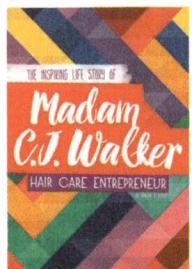
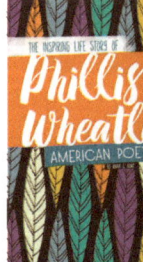

Further Reading

Caravantes, Peggy. *Daughters of Two Nations.* Missoula, Mont.: Mountain Press Publishing Company, 2013.

Lowery, Linda. *Native Peoples of the Southwest.* Minneapolis: Lerner Publications, 2015.

Ray, Deborah Kogan. *Paiute Princess: The Story of Sarah Winnemucca.* New York: Frances Foster Books/Farrar Straus Giroux, 2012.

Internet Sites

Use FactHound to find Internet sites related to this book. All of the sites on FactHound have been researched by our staff.

Here's all you do:

Visit www.facthound.com

Type in this code: 9780756551674

Source Notes

Page 7, line 9: Gae Whitney Canfield. *Sarah Winnemucca of the Northern Paiutes*. Norman: University of Oklahoma Press, 1983, pp. 60–61.

Page 8, sidebar, line 5: Ibid., p. 61.

Page 8, sidebar, line 12: Ibid., p. 62.

Page 13, line 1: Sarah Winnemucca. *Life Among the Piutes: Their Wrongs and Claims*. Reno: University of Nevada Press, 1994 (first published 1883 by G.P. Putnam's Sons), p. 5.

Page 14, line 21: Ibid., p. 25.

Page 17, line 11: Ibid., p. 7.

Page 18, line 4: Sally Springmeyer Zanjani. *Sarah Winnemucca*. Lincoln: University of Nebraska Press, 2001, p. 18.

Page 20, line 10: *Life Among the Piutes: Their Wrongs and Claims*, p. 29.

Page 31, line 17: *Sarah Winnemucca*, p. 61.

Page 32, line 8: *Sarah Winnemucca of the Northern Paiutes*, p. 25.

Page 36, line 1: Ibid., p. 30.

Page 42, line 1: *Sarah Winnemucca*, p. 72.

Page 44, line 8: Ibid., p. 76.

Page 44, line 15: *Sarah Winnemucca of the Northern Paiutes*, p. 42.

Page 47, line 8: *Life Among the Piutes: Their Wrongs and Claims*, p. 78.

Page 50, line 1: Ibid., pp. 86–87.

Page 51, line 15: *Sarah Winnemucca*, p. 111.

Page 51, line 22: *Life Among the Piutes: Their Wrongs and Claims*, p. 65.

Page 52, line 15: Ibid., p. 82.

Page 54, line 6: Ibid., p. 85.

Page 62, line 9: *Sarah Winnemucca of the Northern Paiutes*, p. 107.

Page 70, line 21: *Life Among the Piutes: Their Wrongs and Claims*, p. 164.

Page 72, line 6: Ibid., p. 164.

Page 73, line 2: Ibid., p. 193.

Page 73, line 17: Ibid., p. 205.

Page 75, line 11: Ibid., p. 239.

Page 78, line 12: Ibid., p. 222.

Page 79, line 7: *Sarah Winnemucca of the Northern Paiutes*, pp. 163–164.

Page 79, line 19: Ibid., p. 167.

Page 80, line 14: *Life Among the Piutes: Their Wrongs and Claims*, p. 236.

Page 82, line 4: *Sarah Winnemucca of the Northern Paiutes*, p. 187.

Page 86, line 17: *Life Among the Piutes: Their Wrongs and Claims*, p. 207.

Page 93, line 21: *Sarah Winnemucca*, p. 259.

Page 94, line 19: Ibid., p. 267.

Select Bibliography

Ashby, Ruth, and Deborah Gore Ohrn. *Herstory: Women Who Changed the World.*
New York: Viking, 1995.

Bush, Don. "The History of the Crookedest Short Line in America, the Virginia and Truckee Railroad." 4 May 2016.
http://www.vcnevada.com/history/Vnthist.htm

Canfield, Gae Whitney. *Sarah Winnemucca of the Northern Paiutes.*
Norman: University of Oklahoma Press, 1983.

Egan, Ferol. *Sand in a Whirlwind: The Paiute Indian War of 1860.*
Reno: University of Nevada Press, 2003,

Kilcup, Karen, ed. *Native American Women's Writing: c. 1800–1924: An Anthology.*
Malden, Mass.: Blackwell Publishers, 2000.

Kilcup, Karen L., ed. *Nineteenth-Century American Women Writers: A Critical Reader.*
Malden, Mass.: Blackwell Publishers, 1998.

Nevada Writers Hall of Fame: Sarah Winnemucca. 4 May 2016. http://guides.library.unr.edu/nvwriters-hall-of-fame/winnemucca-1993

Ritchie, Joy, and Kate Ronald, eds. *Available Means: An Anthology of Women's Rhetoric(s).* Pittsburgh: University of Pittsburgh Press, 2001.

Senier, Siobhan. *Voices of American Indian Assimilation and Resistance: Helen Hunt Jackson, Sarah Winnemucca, and Victoria Howard.*
Norman: University of Oklahoma Press, 2001.

Walker, Cheryl. *Indian Nation: Native American Literature and Nineteenth Century Nationalisms.* Durham, N.C.: Duke University Press, 1997.

Winnemucca, Sarah. *Life Among the Piutes: Their Wrongs and Claims.* Edited by Mrs. Horace Mann, and printed for the author. New York: G.P. Putnam's Sons and by the author, 1883. http://digital.library.upenn.edu/women/winnemucca/piutes/piutes.html

Zanjani, Sally Springmeyer. *Sarah Winnemucca.*
Lincoln: University of Nebraska Press, 2001.

Index

Academy of Notre Dame 36–37
Argasse, Julius 60
arrest 60

Bannock War 68, 69, 70, 73, 80, 82, 83
Bartlett, Edward 57–59, 65
Bateman, Calvin 59
Bernard, Reuben 69–70
birth 11
Bonnifield, Mac 60
Bonsall, Jacob 20
Bureau of Indian Affairs 6, 62, 77
Butler, Louisa 59

Camp Harney 62, 67
Camp McDermit 5–6, 7, 51, 53, 55, 57–58, 91
Captain Jim 29, 77
Century of Dishonor, A (Helen Hunt Jackson) 9
Chapin, Alice 97
childhood 12, 16–17, 18–20
clothing 19–20, 51, 79, 85–86
Comstock Lode 27

death 99
divorce 59, 65
Donner Party 15–16, 19
Douglas, Henry 6–7, 8, 9

education 8, 12, 20–21, 26–27, 36–37
Elma (sister) 18, 25, 26, 29, 31, 34, 36, 37, 39, 82, 84, 98

Frémont, John Charles 13–14

Ghost Dance movement 98
Grant, Ulysses S. 62
Green, John 62

Hayes, Rutherford B. 77, 78, 81–82
health 19, 98, 99
Hopkins, Lewis 82–84, 85, 97–98
Howard, Oliver 70, 72, 80–81

interpreter work 6, 41, 42, 60, 70, 78, 81, 93

Jackson, Helen Hunt 9
Jerome, Aaron 50, 52–53

Kuyuidika-a band 11, 13, 15, 22, 28, 70

lecture tours 75, 77, 79, 84–86, 91, 92, 93
Lee (brother) 84
Life Among the Piutes: Their Wrongs and Claims (book) 86–88
Life at a Glance 23

Malheur Reservation 60–62, 62–65, 67–68, 80
Mann, Mary Peabody 84–85, 86, 95
marriages 39–40, 58, 65, 83
Marshall, James 20
Mary (sister) 18, 20, 21, 47
McElroy, James N. 7
Mexican War 14, 17
Mud Lake massacre 46–47

name 11, 26, 65
Natchez (brother) 18, 29, 32, 49, 50, 52, 54, 55, 59, 70, 77, 78, 93, 94, 97, 100
Nugent, Hugh 50
Numaga (cousin) 29, 30, 31–32, 34

Ormsby, Lizzie 25, 26
Ormsby, Margaret 25, 26, 29
Ormsby, William 25, 29, 30–31, 32

Paiute people 5–6, 11–12, 14–15, 18, 19, 27–28, 30, 31–32, 39, 40, 41, 44, 45–46, 49–50, 51, 53–55, 60–61, 62–65, 67, 70, 73, 75, 91–92, 93, 94, 98, 99
Parrish, Annie 61, 65
Parrish, Charles 65
Parrish, Samuel 60, 62
Peabody, Elizabeth 84–85, 94, 95, 96–97
Peabody Indian School 94, 98
petition 86, 91
presidential meeting 68, 78
Pyramid Lake Reservation 6, 49, 59, 84, 91–92, 100
Pyramid Lake War 30, 31–32, 34

Index cont.

ranching work 20–22
rescue mission 70–73
Rinehart, William 62–64, 65, 67–68, 88

Satwaller, Joseph 65
Schurz, Carl 78, 80, 82
Scott, Hiram 20
scouting work 70, 82
Seward, Dudley 53, 55
Smith, John 82, 99
Snyder, Mr. 34, 39–40
stage performances 42–45
statue 100

teaching work 61, 81, 93, 94, 96–97
Tom (brother) 18, 84
Truckee (grandfather) 11, 13, 14, 15, 17, 18, 19, 20, 22, 25–26, 31, 34–36
Tuboitonie (mother) 11, 18, 19, 21, 47

U.S. Congress 91, 92

Victor, Benjamin 100

Walker River Reservation 6
Washoe people 29
Wasson, Warren 49
Wilbur, James 74–75, 80
Winnemucca (father) 11, 18, 19, 22, 27, 31, 34, 40–41, 42–43, 44, 45, 55, 59, 60, 62, 65, 70, 72–73, 77, 78, 84
Wounded Knee massacre 98–99
Wovoka (Paiute leader) 98

Yakima Reservation 73–75, 78

CRITICAL THINKING USING THE COMMON CORE

1. Sarah Winnemucca spent her life trying to help the Paiute people, but many of her efforts met with failure. Why do you think they didn't succeed? Support your answer with evidence from the text. (Key Ideas and Details)

2. Sarah felt as if she was trying to live in two worlds—the Paiute world and in white American society. Do you think she was ever fully accepted in either world? Why or why not? (Key Ideas and Details)

3. Sarah lived during a time when women in general and American Indian women in particular had few rights and career options. How would her life have been different had she lived today? (Integration of Knowledge and Ideas)